SCRIPTORIUM

THE NATIONAL POETRY SERIES

The National Poetry Series was established in 1978 to ensure the publication of five collections of poetry annually through five participating publishers. Publication is funded annually by the Lannan Foundation, Amazon Literary Partnership, Barnes & Noble, the Poetry Foundation, the PG Family Foundation and the Betsy Community Fund, Joan Bingham, Mariana Cook, Stephen Graham, Juliet Lea Hillman Simonds, William Kistler, Jeffrey Ravetch, Laura Baudo Sillerman, and Margaret Thornton. For a complete listing of generous contributors to the National Poetry Series, please visit www.nationalpoetryseries.org.

2015 COMPETITION WINNERS

Scriptorium
By Melissa Range of Appleton, Wisconsin.
Chosen by Tracy K. Smith. Publisher: Beacon Press.

Not on the Last Day, But on the Very Last
By Justin Boening of Iowa City, Iowa.
Chosen by Wayne Miller. Publisher: Milkweed Editions.

The Wug Test
By Jennifer Kronovet of New York, New York.
Chosen by Eliza Griswold. Publisher: Ecco.

Trébuchet
By Danniel Schoonebeek of Brooklyn, New York.
Chosen by Kevin Prufer. Publisher: University of Georgia Press.

The Sobbing School
By Joshua Bennett of Yonkers, New York.
Chosen by Eugene Gloria. Publisher: Penguin.

scriptorium

POEMS

MELISSA RANGE

Beacon Press
Boston

Beacon Press
Boston, Massachusetts
www.beacon.org

Beacon Press books
are published under the auspices of
the Unitarian Universalist Association of Congregations.

19 18 17   8 7 6 5 4 3 2

This book is printed on acid-free paper that meets the uncoated paper
ANSI/NISO specifications for permanence as revised in 1992.

Text design and composition by Wilsted & Taylor Publishing Services

Library of Congress Cataloging-in-Publication Data

Names: Range, Melissa, author.
Title: Scriptorium : poems / Melissa Range.
Description: Boston : Beacon Press, [2016]
Identifiers: LCCN 2015049944 (print) | LCCN 2016005063 (ebook)
     | ISBN 9780807094440 (pbk. : alk. paper) | ISBN 9780807094457
     (ebook)
Classification: LCC PS3618.A646 A6 2016 (print) | LCC PS3618.A646
     (ebook) | DDC 811/.6—dc23
LC record available at http://lccn.loc.gov/2015049944

for my grandmothers

Edith Mae Davis Range
(1907–1995)

Ena Gay Ritchie Pierce
(1921–2007)

CONTENTS

FOREWORD

Each of the poems in *Scriptorium* is a marvel. What may likely strike you on the first read is Range's remarkable facility with form. She moves nimbly, naturally, with comfort and acrobatic delight through the rigors of sonnets, villanelles, anagrams, cento, and the like. She submits joyfully to the whims of rhyme, allowing music to exert its will upon her train of mind, and she does so with such virtuosic ease that you may not even detect it on a first read. But what you will feel more than any of this, I am certain, is an urgent usefulness. These are poems for which form is not an end in itself.

All the many formal commands to which Range's poems gladly bend are in service of something urgent, something having to do with a view of language as a means of survival. In this sense, Range's work reminds me of the phrase "the Living Word," the very thing that ignited the piety of medieval monks; only here it is made up of words that fit in the mouths of "drunkards, / bruisers, goaders, soldiers, / braggers" and their kind. What we say and how we say it, Range urges her readers to see and claim, tells us who we are and who we've been. Our voices mark our time, but they also guard a place for us in time, which is to say, they keep us alive.

Among the things this particular voice seems entrusted with keeping alive is the voice of Appalachia, what the poet claims as her "hillbilly" legacy. Not academically or anthropologically, but as a kind of earnest commemoration, a claiming of kin. And that's not all. Range reanimates Old English, which she assures us "has a word for our kind / of people." And she initiates us into the language of the brightly colored illuminations once meant to serve as vehicles for Christian belief. She casts her eye and ear in every direction, asking, "Must one sing of this?" And answering, "One must."

Traditionally, a scriptorium was a room where monks sat copying manuscripts. The word calls to the sense of what is precious, what must be made and remade, what one could give one's entire life to preserving. How elegant a corollary for the work of the poet, and of this poet in particular, whose most sacred text—the one inspiring the most rapt devotion—is the very vernacular we live, love, grieve, fumble, and forgive in.

Tracy K. Smith

SCRIPTORIUM

VERDIGRIS

Not green as new weeds or crushed juniper,
but a toxic and unearthly green, meet
for inking angel-wings, made from copper sheets
treated with vapors of wine or vinegar,
left to oxidize for the calligrapher.
When it's done, he'll cover calf-skin with a fleet
of knotted beasts in caustic green that eats
the page and grieves the paleographer.
There's copper in my brain, my heart of hearts;
in my blood, an essential mineral.
Too much is poison. Too much air imparts
sickness to the script—once begun, eternal,
its words forever grass in drought. Nor departs
my grief, green and corrosive as a gospel.

LABYRINTH, CHARTRES

Most days the labyrinth's covered
up with folding chairs, but Fridays
it's open even to unbelievers.

Our docent says the labyrinth is not a maze,
that the pilgrim cannot lose her way
coiling toward the center rose.

My pastor friend and I are chaperones,
here to help field-tripping kids
weave the ancient circuit that the masons

made without diversions or dead ends. "One pathway
in, the same path flowering out,"
the docent says, "so that you cannot stray."

My friend instructs our group: "Release,
receive, return." Kids wind along the stone
with palms upturned, seeking the peace

they've been told radiates from the roundels,
the buttresses, the crypts, the statues
of virgins, saints, apostles.

Above us, glaring from the western wall,
Christ the Judge rides on a cloud
of glass, grabbing sinners for his hell,

the righteous for his heaven,
part of the gospel that the craftsmen
fractured into windowpanes.

Shining through the quatrefoil, the wounds
the glaziers cut and set
into Christ's feet and hands,

sun pools blue and scarlet
on the floor, dappling the medallion
where, the legend goes, penitents

and priests walked on their knees.
Now anyone can walk here,
including the faithless, whom God always sees.

The kids circle the path, they pray
as if prayer was a right and not a grace,
they turn upon the way (my friend will say)

of the blest, those who can trust in Christ's name.
He'll remind us, "We're pilgrims, not tourists,"
though the admission is the same.

ASHBURNHAM

With a name like that,
the librarian shouldn't have been surprised

when late night hearth-sparks
kindled mantel-tree and wainscot,

turned the hallways to tinder,
cindered the vellum

already almost too fragile to touch—
an antiquarian's collection

amassed when the monasteries
were dissolved, when books

were flung from scriptoria, torn
parchment used for bootblacks' rags.

A gospel, an epic, a charter aflame,
the only copies thrown from a window

when the librarian could no longer wait
for the bucket brigade;

the next morning, schoolboys
pocketed the black and buckled scraps.

The poem about the seafaring hero,
bound into a larger volume

of monster-tales and marvels,
smoked as if from dragon-fire,

parts of the tale already worm-eaten,
and though the restorationists

cleaned and pinned the leaves—
fire-brittle, water-warped—

to a line to dry, the story kept
disintegrating, its margins

crumbling further at each touch,
leaving scholars less to copy

of what was already less a copy
than a shadow—the original

unpreserved, irretrievable
the instant the pen quenched

the harp: a smoldering
smothered, a ruin of the tongue.

A SKIFF OF SNOW

Not a boatload but a sift that barely sticks—
the flour sloughed from a rolling pin,
flakes scarce as skiffs in a landlocked state.

In the ballads brought over
with the Scots, women pine for word
of a lover or a son put out to sea,

a skiff of song scabbing the ground
beneath the willow when they're buried,
beneath the ocean when they're not.

My father on a ladder doesn't sing;
he cusses, banging boards
onto the wind-scrapped barn,

roof half off, wood give out, sky
spitting snow, salvaging
his daddy's daddy's daddy's work—

and before him, even, a man
who didn't row, he walked here
(when this was barely Tennessee)

from New Jersey, and before that,
his father drifted in from Holland,
England, Germany, or France

(the family trees disagree
about which accent
got mangled into mine).

When I left my mountain home to hitch
to cities, I became a hick,
my skiff of twang scuffing the air,

breaking on scoffers' ears like ships
busting on rocks. My granddaddy,
on a job in Cincinnati, drinking up

his paycheck, heard "You must be one of them
hillbillies" soon as he opened his mouth
to ask the baseball score;

he replied, "They is two kinds of people
in this world, hillbillies and sons
of bitches—so what does that make you?"

Then he slugged the feller one,
or got slugged, depending
on who's telling it.

"It's a-skiffin'," we say,
to mean there's not much,
there won't be much, and it'll be gone

in two shakes. It's untelling
where it goes. It's untelling
who'll tell it once it's gone.

ORPIMENT

King's yellow for the King's hair and halo,
mixed if the monastery can't afford
   the shell gold or gold leaf to crown the Lord,
   to work the letters of his name, the Chi-Ro,
   in trumpet spirals and triquetras, the yellow
   a cheap and lethal burnishing, the hoard
   not gold but arsenic and sulfur. The Word
   curves in compass circles, and again I follow,
   tracing on yellowing vellum my dread
   of this intolerant composition,
   this gold that cannot coexist with lead,
   this God who prefers extermination—
   of false prophets, golden calves, and other gods
   before him—to the wideness of devotion.

NEGATIVE THEOLOGY

I get the call about my grandmother. Maybe it is nothing.
A dark spot on a screen: someone says, "Pray that it is nothing."

On the surgeon's gurney, swaddled in blue—
she's lost how much blood? Like you, she weighs nothing.

Pseudo-Denys says to cast off all images, all qualities of you.
So the sculptor chips marble away into nothing.

The preacher speaks over my grandmother,
half her colon gone, where? He lays hands on nothing.

Unlight, Undark, Unfather, Unson,
Unholy of Unholies—all your names stray into nothing.

In the ICU, she vomits everything but the ice.
Unknowing I know her, a body on its way to nothing.

The star points on the monitor collapse to a line,
Ray of Divine Darkness, ray searing all light to nothing.

Cast off all images, even those that seem flesh, seem true.
"Jesus paid it all," says the preacher. Did he pay it for nothing?

Unmother, Unlover, Undoer, Undone—
like you, she won't have a name. Two can play at nothing.

My mother calls my name, asks me to pray.
When you've got nothing to say, better to say nothing.

KERMES RED

Called crimson, called vermilion—"little worm"
in both the Persian and the Latin, red
eggs for the carmine dye, the insect's brood
crushed stillborn from her dried body, a-swarm
in a bath of oak ash lye and alum to form
the pigment the Germans called Saint John's Blood—
the saint who picked brittle locusts for food,
whose blood became the germ of a crimson storm.
Christ of the pierced thorax and worm-red cloak,
I read your death was once for all, but it's not true:
your kings and bishops command a book,
a beheading, blood for blood, the perfect hue;
thus I, the worm, the Baptist, and the scarlet oak
see all things on God's earth must die for you.

FLAT AS A FLITTER

The way you can crush a bug
or stomp drained cans of Schlitz out on the porch,

the bread when it won't rise,
the cake when it falls after the oven-door slams—

the old people had their way
to describe such things. "But what's a flitter?"

I always asked my granny. And she could never say.
"It's just a flitter. Well, it might be a fritter."

"Then why not say 'fritter'?"
"Shit, Melissa. Because the old people said 'flitter.'"

And she smacked the fried pie into the skillet,
and banged the skillet on the stove,

and shook and turned the pie
till it was on its way to burnt.

Flatter than a flitter, a mountain
when its top's blown off:

dynamited, shaved to the seam,
the spoil pushed into hollers, into streams,

the arsenic slurry caged behind a dam,
teetering above an elementary school.

The old people said "flitter." They didn't live to see
God's own mountain turned

hazard-orange mid-air pond,
a haze of waste whose brightness rivals heaven.

When that I was a little bitty baby,
my daddy drove up into Virginia

to fix strip-mining equipment, everything
to him an innocent machine in need.

On God's own mountain,
poor people drink bad water, and the heart

of the Lord is a seam of coal gouged out
to fuel the light in other places.

The old people didn't live
to give a name to this

kingdom of gravel and blast.
Lay me a hunk of coal

on my flittered tongue
to mark the mountains' graves,

to mark my father's tools
quarrying bread for my baby plate,

to mark my granny slapping dough
as if with God's own flat hand.

NAVAJO CODE TALKERS, WWII

When "turtle" is a tank, a bomber
"chickenhawk," when a Marine's
a kid who's got a mouth on him
his country never cared to learn,
a war can be won. Not
eighty years after the Long Walk
tried to crush it to a stutter
it was pronounced a gift
to the military, this language
they tried to scrub out with lye
or beat out with belts
at Indian boarding schools,
its tones rising and falling
to switch the meaning,
too liquid and difficult
to be broken. When America's
"our mother" and death's
spelled "deer, eye, axe,
tooth, horse" (the cryptograms
never written, always spoken);
when our mother says, "Kill
the Indian to save the man,"

but the killers fail, saved
to live to kill again ("kill"
meaning "kill" from code
to code, codes a child could crack
even if his tongue's in tatters), a war
can be won, but not the one
that matters.

TYRIAN PURPLE

Because a parchment plain and pale as sails
doesn't avail gold ink, and because raw silk
for empresses must not be the shade of chalk,
the murex-fishers bait their wicker creels
with cockles, catch and crush the spiny snails,
then cut the glands out for two drops of milk—
black as clotted blood, expelled when the whelks balk—
to make the putrid dye worth more than pearls.
Fisher of Men, king of the purple page,
before you died, gore matted in your hair,
men flogged you, wound you in a purple rag.
Ascended, enthroned in Caesar's attire,
your mantle now redeems you with his wage:
twelve thousand deaths upon the shores of Tyre.

PIGS (SEE SWINE)

In library books, the rules for subjects long-assigned:
for children's tales, use "pigs"; for grown-ups', prefer "swine."
How now, white sow, on which one will you dine?
Wilbur is "some pig"; Napoleon, some swine.

But there's a book whose pigskin bindings shine
for youth and aged alike, in which the terms align,
pigs and swine; and in its stories, sow supine,
your litter's better bacon in a poke done up with twine.

The Evangels spin a story from the silken ears of swine:
the swineherds eat their lunches by the mountain's steep decline,
by the tombs, where wind's perfumed with marjoram and thyme,
with the sweet smell of the cedars, the sweet reek of the swine;

and by the tombs, a bruised man roots for acorns, as benign
in his iron fetters as the Son of Man, the Vine,
who withers branches, makes blood out of wine.
The shackled shouting man's a temple with no shrine,

or two thousand shrines, and every one maligned
by other gods, other incarnations, so this text opines:
gods unclean as hordes of hogs, scores of swine,
hooves divided, eyes savage, tails serpentine.

O lardlings, your Lord cometh, and you know not his design.
He sails across still waters and his lips are caked with brine.
Piglets, he will not give this generation a sign,
unless that sign be read in demons, in the bristling flesh of swine.

For "swine," see "pneuma," see "spirit," see the soul unconfined.
See incarnation thistle-pink with hock and flank and rind.
See madman counsel madman, chapter, verse, and line.
See spirits seek for bodies, and see the spirits find.

See the book consign the flock, loin and heart and mind,
to a tumble through the salty sky, their transport undefined.
Over the cliff, swine see pigs, and pigs see swine—
legion, yet one: porcine, insane, divine.

OFERMOD

Now, tell me one difference," my sister says,
"between Old English and New English."

   Well, Old English has a word for our kind
   of people: *ofermod*, literally

   "overmind," or "overheart,"
   or "overspirit," often translated

   "overproud." When the warrior Byrhtnoth,
   overfool, invited the Vikings

   across the ford at Maldon to fight
   his smaller troop at closer range,

   his overpride proved deadlier
   than the gold-hilted and file-hard

   swords the poet gleefully describes—
   and aren't we like that, high-strung

and *ofermod* as our daddy and granddaddies
and everybody else

in our stiff-necked mountain town,
always with something stupid to prove,

doing 80 all the way to the head of the holler,
weaving through the double lines;

splinting a door-slammed finger
with popsicle sticks and electrical tape;

not filling out the forms for food stamps
though we know we qualify.

Sister, I've seen you cuss rivals,
teachers, doctors, bill collectors,

lawyers, cousins, strangers
at the red light or the Walmart;

you start it, you finish it,
you everything-in-between-it,

whether it's with your fists,
or a two-by-four, or a car door,

and it doesn't matter that your foe's
stronger, taller, better armed.

I don't tell a soul when I'm down
to flour and tuna and a half-bag of beans,

so you've not seen me do without
just to do without, just for spite

at them who told us,
"It's a sin to be beholden."

If you're Byrhtnoth
lying gutted on the ground,

speechifying at the troops he's doomed,
then I'm the idiot campaigner

fighting beside his hacked-up lord
instead of turning tail,

insisting, "Mind must be the harder,
heart the keener, spirit the greater,

as our strength lessens."
Now, don't that sound familiar?

We've bought it all our lives
as it's been sold by drunkards,

bruisers, goaders, soldiers,
braggers with a single code:

you might be undermined, girl,
but don't you never be *undermod*.

LAMPBLACK

Black as a charred plum-stone, as a plume
from a bone-fire, as a flume of ravens
  startled from a battle-tree—this lantern resin
  the monk culls from soot to quill the doom
  and glory of the Lord won't fade. The grime
  of letters traced upon the riven
  calf-skin gleams dark as fresh ash on a shriven
  penitent, as heaven overawing time.
  World's Glim, Grim Cinderer, is it sin
  or history or a whimsied hex that burns
  all life to tar? We are dust, carbon
  spilled out from your Word, a lamp overturned
  into the pit of pitch beneath your pen,
  the inkhorn filled before the world was born.

FORTUNES OF MEN

When a youngun's born,
only God, the Anointer, knows
what the winters have in store:

the Lord is on him like a duck
on a junebug; the Lord tracks her
like a trained coonhound

and orders fate and fortune
just as it pleases him to do.
To each he gives a dab:

one will wring enough of chickens' necks
to get to where she hates
the smell of chicken and dumplings.

One will work the dirt; one will punch
a timecard; one will be too agitated
to hold down any job for long.

It is one's doom to get switched
all through life. (The Measurer makes
trees bear switches in their seasons.)

Another will rev his Dodge
around the lake of a Saturday night,
lit up on Old Crow,

but will never wreck, never run
some innocent off the road;
that lucky one will fall

into the yard and pass out
safely in the grass that God,
the Sower, made to be his bed.

A certain one mixes Xanax and methadone;
his veins shake him to a youthful death,
and his mother forgets for a moment

her husband's dealings with some skank,
her slide into the yellow Camaro
of some high-school boy;

her own name is weary to her.
One must wear the badge,
must kick in the doors

of pot growers and meth heads;
and one must get his door kicked in.
So has the Enforcer planned it,

to whom men must give thanks.
A certain one must get a job
(the only job for miles around,

as the Lord, the Overseer,
ordains) dynamiting
mountains to get at the coal;

another one must use the coal
to heat her stove; another one
must use the coal to heat

her curling iron. A certain one
gets rich converting cheap land,
pure water, cheap labor into rayon.

One must fix a supper every night;
and one must give the supper away
to them worse off just down the pike.

One is good at figures; one is good
at nailing boards; one is good
at telling tales; one is good

at meanness; one is good
at making do; one is good
at taking rednecks for a ride.

Must one sing of this? One must:
to a certain one is given the harp,
which like the sword does not depart

from this land; and that one must
praise God for the sorrow
he creates. So the mighty Lord,

the Regulator, deals out to all
across the surface of the earth—
and also in these hills, which he makes

to crumble, as befits his notions,
and his plenty, and his mercies,
which one cannot resist, but does.

NICODEMUS MAKES AN ANALYSIS

Thesis: That the body cannot repent
of its own nativity, cannot re-form,
like water can, into clouds or ice
or tides. That the body can only pull

forward: does not Qoheleth say
the silver cord snaps, the golden bowl
crashes, the jar is shattered at the spring?
So I have it in my annotations: the body

ages, bones raging to return to crushed stone,
decomposing leaves. The living body,
by the time it's old, must be full of earth
ground into its pores—from decades

of work or play or travel; or from inertia,
bands of dust settling, as onto bookshelves,
into layers of marrow—so fertile, flowers
could bloom from anyone's eyes or mouth.

Grass withers, flowers fall, writes the Prophet.
And eloquently, I might add—not like this youth
who can't construct a story with any unity
of metaphor, who weaves and warps

his plainclothes homilies without regard
for the listener's sensibilities. And clarity?
He quips a snippet from the Psalmist—
out of context, to be sure—and slaps it on

his ramblings as a patch. But I digress
from my topic. Thesis: That the body
is only made for one space, one duration.
On the shore, the spines and ribs of what were fish—

tiny harps, the music drummed out of them
by the sea. Water, then salt.
Is an old man's body any different?
Methuselah, who outlived even *rocks*,

did so in the one body; Enoch, who sidestepped
death, did so in the one body. Thesis:
That our bodies are too ravaged in their wanderings,
their meal-takings and slumberings, to desire

more than one gestation. *Is this the way*
you think? he said. *The way you see?*
And left me no time to reply, to show him
my sources, all I have collected. Years

of marginalia and notations—all disseminated,
as by a bellows-blast. My life's work!
He would have nothing of it, but kept up
his discourse. No data, no statistics—his logic

one of circles circling circles, his proofs
spinning and arcing, never lighting: phylacteries
opened, their frail contents flown.
I sat. I studied the fire. And I followed,

not his argument, but his gestures, his fingers
tricking my vision in the shadows. Such fingers—
I cannot sleep for thinking about them, how thin
the skin on the tips, as if they were made of paper.

Thesis: That each of his fingers is a page
from a water-sodden book—the meanings
delicate, on the verge of being torn apart,
rendered unreadable. That his face

is the face that the wind wears when it carries rain
or scratches the thunder purple and blue.
Whoever watches the wind will not plant,
whoever looks at the clouds will not reap.

I forget who said that. And I'm no longer sure
which citations I might wish to keep: my body
of work immaterial, like water condensed
to mere conjecture—what once filled

a river, a cup, a womb, nothing but air.
Hypothesis: That my books are wrong—
or riddled with misprints, faulty definitions.
Come morning, I must make a few revisions.

BIBLIA PAUPERUM

This fold-out triptych, gilded comic book,
is mostly images, sufficient
for the poor to understand;

Gothic-scripted reds and blues and golds
provide the bit of text the pastor's flock
can't read and aren't allowed to touch.

In the middle panel, the Magi give
their patrons' wages to the child,
who doesn't know what money is;

on the left, Abner switches to David's side
after stabbing David's men
(a gold staff makes an enemy a friend);

on the right, Sheba offers Solomon gold
(what is gold to a rich man but a boring story
he still likes hearing over and over?).

On a different page, the first priest,
Melchizadek, hands bread to Abraham,
while in another panel manna falls,

gilt-outlined globes Moses plucks from the sky
and gives to the people, who have nothing
but a leader and their shared hunger;

in the center panel, the Last Supper,
the cup is gold, the bread is gold,
and the bread's not for the body

but the spirit. The colors are so garish,
even the poor can understand
(not the poor in spirit but the poor

in fact) what illuminates
Christ's dough-white face—the waste
of love, the supper gone cold without a taste.

MINIUM

The monk stipples the page with convoluted trails
of lead toasted rust-red, brick-red, the color
first used for rubric and for miniature.
Three thousand tiny dots prick the initials,
as if the text itself were pierced with nails,
red edging each green, black, or yellow letter
to embolden the story of Christ's dolor
and his murder, his earthborn travails.
Some letters aren't filled in. The red dots, wrapped
obsessive round the page, perhaps so vexed
their maker that the monk just stopped—
or else he didn't know what happened next
and so kept dotting, blotting, dotting, trapped
inside Christ's body, a bloody outline with no text.

ANAGRAM: SEE A GRAY PINE

in memory, Ena Gay Pierce

See a gray pine in January that ought to be green
See me pining for a gray-headed one
See the gray shale with its pines unpinned
See a pin from her pincushion under the bed
See a gray cookpot of pinto beans
See gray hairs caught in an old bobby pin
See me gray, still pining
Whose gray hills are these, unpined?
Gray crone: thine

SOLIDUS OF THE EMPRESS IRENE, AD 797–802

Numismatists know it's just a coin
despite its name, related to the Latin

for safe—*salvus*—
and entire—*sollus*—

for the safety money brings,
for the entirety it becomes to kings,

homeowners, parents, execs,
all of us whose bills are due before our checks.

It's not an icon, though the gold's the same
as the gold membrane

surrounding Mary, Jesus, Elijah, John,
all constellated around Irene

on this gray wall, Irene the iconodule,
who made icons the center of her rule

after she stole the throne from Constantine
the 6th, her son, whom she had blinded, an icon

with his painted eyes scratched out. Irene's
four ringlets clink like strings of coins,

her eyes are coins, her tunic's printed
with tiny coins. She glints new-minted

as a newfound sun or a new-named land,
though she won't spend,

and though she's resistant
to corrosion, she's so thin she could be bent

by hand. It's not an icon but an impress,
though the gold's the same. Less

use than a penny in the reaches
of my pocketbook, than God in the clutches

of an unbeliever,
but she'll rule this wall forever,

deposed Irene iconodule,
who finished her poor life in exile, carding wool.

INCARNATIONAL THEOLOGY

after Jürgen Moltmann

"God suffers in us, where love suffers,"
writes the theologian of the cross,
the fate awaiting all God's lovers.

You are my beloved, says the Father
as his dove rips through clouds to bless
the Son with suffering. In us, where love suffers,

Christ's ache throbs closer than a brother's—
stabbing my breasts, my thighs, his loneliness,
the fate awaiting all God's lovers.

God takes on flesh and thinks he'll smother.
Reeling, obsessed, his heart a wilderness,
God's a mess, suffering in me as I suffer

over a torn leaf, a tore-up man, the others
I've tried to love, shorn to the bone and luckless
as the Son. What fate's awaiting all the lovers

who dwell in me as migraines, as a stutter
in the veins, whose loss grows in me like grass?
God suffers them gladly. In us, love suffers:
it's the grace awaiting all God's lovers.

WOAD

"Every word of the Lord written by the scribe
is a wound on Satan's body." —CASSIODORUS, 6TH CENTURY

Once thought lapis on the carpet page, mined
from an Afghani cave, this new-bruise clot
in the monk's ink pot grew from Boudicca's plot—
a naturalized weed from a box of black seeds found
with a blue dress in a burial mound.
Knobs of leaves that reeked like cabbage rot,
steeped and strained for Britons' battle paint, wrought
the Gospels' splotched knotwork, the monk's dyed hand.
Gouged with quills, woad-hued blots beneath your hide,
Lucifer, who can understand your blues?
I can: the Lord invades my piece of sod
to set up a scriptorium, introduce
true indigo, and build a Roman road;
he knots my blue veins till I can't refuse.

HIT

Hit was give to me,
the old people's way of talking,
and hit's a hit

sometimes. Sometimes hit
is plumb forgot
and I drop the "h"

that starts hillbilly,
hellfire, hateful,
hope. Sometimes hit

hits the back of my teeth
and fights hits way out
for hit's been around

and hit's tough:
hit's Old English,
hit's Middle, hit's country,

hit will hit on you
all day long
if you'll let hit.

When I hit the books
they tried to hit
hit out of me,

but hit's been hit
below the belt
and above and hit

still ain't hit
the sack. Sometimes
you can hit hit

like a nail on the head,
and sometimes hit
hits back.

VERNACULAR THEOLOGY:
MECHTHILD OF MAGDEBURG

In the muddy stretch between the market and the church
a song flows from a tavern, and it soaks the roads

in melted gold; a girl picks flowers from the ditches,
and her lover's kisses whisper in each broken stem;

the bells for vespers burn a gasp of sun
into the moon, into my chest, into the host.

And all of this happens in German—from my tongue,
German overspills, light lilting from itself onto the water.

When I pray, the prayer is German; when I love,
I love in German, and thus my Lover's mouth replies.

And when I, weak as a wind-stroked dove,
love into silence, my silences are German,

and they are so nicely honeycombed.
I know no Latin. Nor does the girl who reads

the letters of her lover's name in every coiling cloud;
or the maids who wash and kiss, with oils, the dead;

or my sisters who wind their thumbs
with thread as red as wine-drenched bread.

My Lover bestowed Latin—a tabernacle, a gilded chest—
to some servants; they write, tight-lipped,

the Bridegroom from his bed into a crypt.
They would lock him in their books and eat the key.

But he kissed German into me. He sings,
a burning mountain; he aches, a churning tree.

So a lofty crag yearns into stones: for he desires
to shatter into every tongue, not die, unbroken,

inside one. The end of Latin is where I begin,
where my Lover takes his shape. On the page,

in my mouth, such sweetness, crushed—
O German, you taste like a grape.

TO SWAN

If you won't swear, you'll have to swan.
Nana did it all day long.
She swanned at weather, swanned at news.
Her Bible told her it was wrong

to swear an oath before the Lord.
Granddaddy Range had said so, too
(when she was a foul-mouthed bride
and their marriage was new),

and so she swanned and cleaned,
swanned and canned, swanned and fanned,
while across town, Ena swore.
I swear she never swanned;

she swore she never cussed.
When Nana was in the nursing home,
her mind stretched big enough for anything,
she loved a good *fuck you* and a good *goddamn*.

Ena (who wouldn't stop her swearing
for another dozen years)
sat by Nana, didn't mutter even *shit*,
didn't drop a goddamn tear,

but looked at Nana's swan-white hair,
then looked at me, then at her hands,
as if by looking she could find
words as calm as swans, as grand.

ULTRAMARINE

Beyond the blue scum sea, miners assault
lazurite and pyrite, a blue-gold beam,
    pry from limestone caverns the lapis seam
    for the shade that painters' patrons so exalt
    to hem the Virgin's mantle, foam the Vault
    where she's fixed like a lodestar or a gem.
Mixed with wax and turpentine, by the dram
    this powdered stone costs more than gold or salt.
Stella Maris, Blue-Eyed Lady of the Whale-
    Road, God tore your veil into the seas
    that hide Leviathan's blue fluke and flail,
    the skies that hold the sailor's compass
    made of ice-trussed stars. You're vessel of the swell,
    and all the deep will be your swaddling clothes.

CROOKED AS A DOG'S HIND LEG

Yanking my lank hair into dog-ears,
my granny frowned at my cowlick's
revolt against the comb, my part

looking like a dog's shank
no matter what she did, crooked
as the dogtrot path

out the mountain county I left
with no ambitions to return,
rover-minded as my no-count granddaddy, crooking

down switchbacks that crack the earth
like the hard set of the mouth
women are born with where I'm from.

Their faces have a hundred ways to say
"Don't go off," "Your place is here,"
"Why won't you settle down?"—

and I ignored them all like I was one
of their ingrate sons (jobless, thankless,
drugged up, petted to death), meandering

like a scapegrace in a ballad,
as a woman with no children likes to do,
as a woman with crooked roots knows she can.

"When you coming home?" my granny
would ask when I called, meaning "to visit"
but meaning more "to stay,"

and how could I tell her
that the creeks crisscrossing
our tumbledown ridges

are ropes trying to pull my heart straight
when it's a crooked muscle,
its blood crashing in circles?

Why should I tell her
that since I was a mop-headed infant
and leapt out of my baby bed,

I've been bent on skipping
the country, glad as a chained-up hound
until I slipped my rigging?

What could I say but "I'll be home Christmas,"
what could I hear but "That's a long time,"
what could I do but bless

the crooked teeth in my head
and dog the roads that lead all ways
but one?

ALL CREATION WEPT

And not just those disciples
whom he loved, and not just
his mother; for all creation

was his mother, if he shared
his cells with worms and ferns
and whales, silt and spiderweb,

with the very walls of his crypt.
Of all creation, only he slept,
the rest awake and rapt with grief

when love's captain leapt
onto the cross, into an abyss
the weather hadn't dreamt.

Hero mine the beloved,
cried snowflakes, cried the moons
of unknown planets, cried the thorns

in his garland, the nails bashed
through his bones, the spikes of dry grass
on the hillside, dotted with water

and with blood—real tears,
and not a trick of rain-light
blinked and blurred onto a tree

so that the tree seems wound
in gold. It was not wound
in gold or rain but in a rapture

of salt, the wood splintering
as he splintered when he wept
over Lazarus, over Jerusalem,

until his sorrow became his action,
his grief his victory—
until his tears became a rupture

in nature, all creation
discipled to his suffering
on the gilded gallows-tree,

the wood which broke beneath the weight
of love, though it had no ears to hear
him cry out, and no eyes to see.

THE GIANTS' SWORD MELTS

Beowulf, 1605–1617

If all metal once were water,
if all water once could cut the skin—

if the edge could withstand the blood,
could turn aside its face,

could still ask, *now can you guess my name?*,
would it ask it in the giants' tongue?

Or in the tongue of ice, of layers
of glaciers melted to a silver point,

a blade of barrow-light, a drop
of sun that once shone on a tale

of men as tall as trees? And like trees
they towered terribly, like trees

they stretched to scathe the sky,
this sky of scalding waves.

Who put you there, ice-brand
heavy as a mother's tongue

when she has lost her son?
Who scratched a flood onto your hilt?

Who committed to your melted steel
a spell, a tale terrific strange

in runes that once were songs,
the singers' voices fetters of frost,

the script not the real story,
the real story water-bands loosening, lost?

GOLD LEAF

the Gospel Book of Otto III, ca. 10th century

Shines forth from the vellum this film of sun,
the precious metal pounded thick as air,
  then bound to the page with gesso or with glair—
  more than one hundred leaves of gold from one
  ducat. Otto, on the gold-leaf throne
  which he commissioned—servant of Christ, ruler
  of the world—surveys his gilded empire,
  and the hand of God adjusts his crown.
  O Christ, how I have loved you, with my heart shut
  like an emperor's fist or a golden door,
  a Bible with its pages locked up tight.
  In my poverty I sought a poor God to adore,
  a love I could buy with my widow's mite.
  But this is not a Bible for the poor.

CENTO: NATURAL THEOLOGY

Hildegard of Bingen, 12th century

Partly like the sun and partly like the air,
the earth—just like a body
if it had no bones. As if by veins
it is held together so it does not crumble.
Like a lamb sucking milk, the plants
suck up the green; place the emerald
in their mouth and the spirit will revive,
a fire of burning mountains
which is difficult to put out,
like the thunder's eye. It cannot be caught.
It ministers to those who bear it,
coming from the mystery of God
like limestone from stone, one drop
of dew found on clean grass. All its matter
is from the fresh greenness of the air,
the sharpness of the water, flame
in the heavens. God does not wish to cure it.

REGIONALISM

People mock the South wherever I pass through.
It's so racist, so backward, so NASCAR.
I don't hate it, but they all do.

As if they themselves marched out in blue,
they're still us-themming it about the Civil War,
mocking the South, wherever it is (they've never passed through).

It's a formless humid place with bad food (except for BBQ)—
the grits, slick boiled peanuts, sweet tea thick as tar.
I don't hate it, but they all do,

though they love Otis Redding, Johnny Cash, the B-52s.
The rest of it can go ahead and char.
People mock my Southern mouth wherever I pass through,

my every "might could have" and "fixin' to,"
my flattened vowels that make "fire" into "far."
I don't hate how I talk, where I'm from, but they all do

their best to make me. It's their last yahoo
in a yahooing world of smear, slur, and mar.
People mock the South, its past. They're never through.
I'm damned if I don't hate it, and damned if I do.

SCRIPTORIUM

Before the stepwork and the fretwork,
before the first wet spiral leaves the brush,
   before the plucking of the geese's quills,
   before the breaking of a thousand leads,

   before the curving limbs and wings
   of hounds, cats, and cormorants
   knot into letters, before the letters knot
   into the Word, Eadfrith ventures from his cell,

   reed basket on his arm, past Cuthbert's grave,
   past the stockyard where the calves' cries bell,
   and their blood illuminates the dirt as ink
   on vellum, across the glens and woods

   to gather woad and lichens, to the shores
   to gather shells. The earth, not the cell,
   is his scriptorium, where he might see
   the interlace of branch and twig and leaf;

how green bleeds brown when fields are plowed;
how green banks blue where grass gives way to sea;
how blue twists into white in swirling lines
purling through the water and the sky.

Before the skinning of a hundred calves,
before the stretching and the scraping of their hides,
before the boiling vinegar, the toasting lead,
the bubbling orpiment and verdigris,

before the glair cracks from the egg,
before the monk perfects his recipe
(egg white, oak-gall, iron salt, mixed
in a tree-stump, some speculate)

to make the pigments glorious to the Lord,
before Eadfrith's fingers are permanently stained
the colors of his world—crimson, emerald,
cerulean, gold—outside the monastery walls,

in the village, with its brown hounds
spooking yellow cats stalking green-black birds,
on the purple-bitten lips of peasants
his gospel's corruption already sings forth

in vermilion ink, firebrands on a red calf's hide—
though he'll be dead before the Vikings sail,
and two centuries of men and wars
will pass before his successor Aldred

pierces Eadfrith's text with thorn,
ash, and all the other angled letters
of his gloss. Laced between the lines of Latin,
the vernacular proclaims, in one dull tint,

a second illumination,
of which Eadfrith was not unaware:
this good news is for everyone,
like language, like color, like air.

SHELL WHITE

The monk grinds bleach from mollusk-carapace,
pestles his basket of beach-combed sea-crumbs
so limed hides might beam brighter for the Lamb.
Before he paints incipit, interlace,
he blenches before the page as if it were the face
that he might hope to glimpse in prayer, numb
within the blizzard of love that strikes dumb
the heart, shell-shocked before the story's grace.
Eyefull of Snow, Dazzling Blank—
I believed you once the union of all light
and pled the searing of my eyes. Then I blinked.
My wool-puller, my white-hot blind spot,
I'm washed up, shelled out, your thankless monk,
or else the page you'd scour, whitewash, illuminate.

NOTES

"Ashburnham"

On October 23, 1731, many singular volumes and manu-
scripts in the Cotton Library, including the only extant copy
of *Beowulf*, were irreparably damaged or destroyed in the
Ashburnham House fire. Some of the poem's details are from
*A Report from the Committee Appointed to View the Cottonian
Library . . . [signed by] W. Whiston*. Printed for R. Williamson
and W. Bowyer, London, 1732. This poem is in memory of
John Miles Foley.

"Negative Theology"

Negative theology, also called apophatic theology, is a branch
of theology that attempts to describe God by negation—to
say what God is *not*, rather than what God *is*. Pseudo-Denys,
a.k.a. Pseudo-Dionysius the Areopagite, was a fifth-century
Neoplatonist thinker and mystical theologian. His *Divine
Names* and *Mystical Theology* are considered foundational
works of negative theology.

"Navajo Code Talkers, WWII"

The quotation "Kill the Indian to save the man" is attributed to Richard Pratt, founder of the Carlisle Indian School in Carlisle, Pennsylvania.

"Pigs (see Swine)"

According to Library of Congress rules, one must classify children's books about pigs under "pigs" and adult books about pigs under "swine"; the terms are not interchangeable.

"Ofermod"

The Old English word *ofermod* appears rarely in the Old English poetic corpus; it most famously describes the warrior Byrhtnoth's foolishly proud (some say arrogant) battle maneuvers in the poem "The Battle of Maldon."

"Fortunes of Men"

This poem takes its inspiration (and its structure, and some of its language) from the Old English poem of the same title.

"Biblia Pauperum"

Literally translated as "Bibles of the Poor," *biblia pauperum* were, in the early medieval period, lavishly illustrated picture-bibles composed primarily of brightly colored illuminations with very little text. Later *biblia pauperum* were woodcuts without coloration. In this poem, the reference is to the illuminated "Golden Bible" (Dutch, fifteenth century).

"Anagram: See a Gray Pine"

This poem follows the Puritan anagram tradition. Anagrams were a popular form among Puritan poets, who often wrote elegies in the form of anagrams of the deceased person's name. In this form, the anagram of the person's name becomes the title of the poem and also recurs thematically throughout the poem. My own anagram on the name "Ena Gay Pierce" follows this convention, with one exception: my poem cheats (as did some Puritan poets!) by using the "s" sound of the letter "c" in "Pierce," rather than the actual letter "c," in order to create the word "see."

"Solidus of the Empress Irene, AD 797–802"

I first encountered this coin at the Art Institute of Chicago, where it was adjacent to a visiting exhibit of art and icons called *Heaven and Earth: Art of Byzantium from Greek Collections*. The solidus is part of the museum's permanent collections.

"Incarnational Theology"

The text quoted in line one of the poem is from Jürgen Moltmann's *The Crucified God: The Cross of Christ as the Foundation and Criticism of Christian Theology* (orig., 1974; Minneapolis: Fortress Press, 1993). This book itself is a translation of *Der gekreuzigte Gott* (Munich: Christian Kaiser Verlag, 1973) by R. A. Wilson and John Bowden.

"Woad"
Boudicca was a legendary British ruler who led an uprising
against the occupying Romans in AD 60 or 61.

"Vernacular Theology: Mechthild of Magdeburg"
Mechthild of Magdeburg was a thirteenth-century German
Beguine. A sort of "lay-religious" group, the Beguines were
women who lived in urban communities and devoted them-
selves to lives of simplicity, chastity, and piety, but who took
no vows and followed no rule. Mechthild wrote of her mys-
tical encounters with God in *The Flowing Light of the God-
head*, considered the first work of mystical theology in the
German vernacular; I draw many of the images in the poem
from Frank Tobin's translation of the book (Mahwah, NJ:
Paulist Press, 1998). The lines "so nicely honeycombed" and
"you taste like a grape" are direct quotations from Tobin's
translation.

"All Creation Wept"
The title of this poem is a translation of the phrase "Weop eal
gesceaft," taken from the Old English poem "The Dream of
the Rood." Thank you to Johanna Kramer for her help with
this poem.

"Cento: Natural Theology"
This poem is constructed of words and phrases taken from
Hildegard of Bingen's *Physica* and *Causae et Curae*, as trans-

lated by Sabina Flanagan in *Secrets of God: Writings of Hildegard of Bingen* (Boston: Shambhala, 1996).

"Scriptorium"

Eadfrith is thought to be the monk who illuminated the Lindisfarne Gospels, c. eighth century; in the tenth century, the priest Aldred inserted his Anglo-Saxon translations of the Latin text between the Latin lines of Eadfrith's work. Aldred's is the oldest extant copy of the Bible translated into English. St. Cuthbert was the saint associated with Lindisfarne at the time the Gospels were illuminated. It is thought that Eadfrith created the pigments used in illuminating the manuscript largely from locally found materials—for example, seashells or eggshells for white, the plant woad for blue, toasted lead for red, carbon for black. I gleaned this information from Michelle P. Brown's books *How Christianity Came to Britain and Ireland, Manuscripts from the Anglo-Saxon Age, Understanding Illuminated Manuscripts: A Glossary of Technical Terms,* and *The Lindisfarne Gospels: Society, Spirituality, and the Scribe.* In this and all other poems dealing with illuminated manuscripts, I made great use of the British Library's online glossary for their Catalogue of Illuminated Manuscripts, as well as a hefty set of reference books on pigments in the reference section of the Savannah College of Art and Design–Atlanta campus library.

ACKNOWLEDGMENTS

A bottomless thank-you to Tracy K. Smith for choosing *Scriptorium* for the National Poetry Series. I'm humbled.

Thank you to Helene Atwan and everyone else at Beacon Press for their warm, enthusiastic, and collaborative way of working with me on this book.

Thank you to the Fine Arts Work Center in Provincetown, Massachusetts, and the Virginia Center for the Creative Arts for residencies that provided much-needed time to work on some of the poems that ended up in this book. And a huge thank-you to Wyatt Prunty and the rest of the good folk at the Sewanee Writers' Conference for believing in me and giving me a place to call home.

Scriptorium began while I was studying theology and, later, working in the theology library at Emory University. Thank you to Brent Strawn, Don Saliers, Steve Kraftchick, and Lyndon Reynolds for teaching fascinating classes that inspired some of the poems in this book. A big thank-you to the cataloguers at Pitts Theology Library (Armin Siedlecki, Denise Hanusek, and Fesseha Nega) for piling so many interesting books about illuminated manuscripts onto my cataloging cart. Another thank-you to Teresa Burk, Grace Dunbar, and Mike Varin at the SCAD–Atlanta library for never monitoring what I was doing during my evening shift at the circulation desk (namely, reading reference books about pigments).

Thank you to these *gesithas* for being my companions in all things Old English: Johanna Kramer, the late John Miles Foley, and the *Beowulfathon* group: Rebecca Mouser, Julie Christenson, Pete Ramey, and Derek Updegraff.

Thank you to these generous and sharp-eyed folks for giving feedback on pieces, parts, and various versions of this manuscript: Danny Anderson, Aliki Barnstone, Heather Dobbins, Gabe Fried, Andrew Hudgins, Mark Jarman, Thomas Kane, Marc McKee, Claire McQuerry, John Nieves, Rachel Richardson, Austin Segrest, and my wonderful dissertation committee at the University of Missouri: Scott Cairns, Frances Dickey, Rabia Gregory, Johanna Kramer, and Alex Socarides.

And thank you to still more fellow poets and friends who have been a part of this manuscript's long evolution: Anne Barngrover, Katy Didden, Donna Forsyth, Pilar Gómez-Ibáñez, Kerry Hill, Kimberly Johnson, Marilyn Kallet, Nadia Kalman, Kathryn Maris, Ginger Pyron, Amanda Rea, Elizabeth Spires, and Johannes Wich-Schwarz.

Thank you to my East Tennessee family, whose musical speech was the first poetry I heard.

Finally, and most importantly, thank you to Austin Segrest: first reader, best reader, best friend, best everything.

CREDITS

Grateful acknowledgment is made to the editors of these publications, in which versions of the following poems first appeared, sometimes under different titles:

32 Poems: "Lampblack"

Birmingham Poetry Review: "Fortunes of Men,"
    "A Skiff of Snow"

Columbia: A Journal of Literature and Art: "Negative
    Theology," "Ashburnham"

CURA: A Literary Magazine of Art and Action: "Navajo
    Code Talkers, WWII"

Ecotone: "Hit"

The Hudson Review: "Pigs (see Swine)"

Image: "Scriptorium," "Minium," "Orpiment,"
    "Kermes Red," "Verdigris"

New England Review: "Incarnational Theology,"
    "All Creation Wept," "Ultramarine," "Tyrian Purple,"
    "Shell White"

The Paris Review: "Nicodemus Makes an Analysis"

Subtropics: "Regionalism"

Tongue: A Journal of Writing and Art: "Cento: Natural
Theology," "Woad" (forthcoming)

Western Humanities Review: "Vernacular Theology: Mech-
thild of Magdeburg" (as "Vernacular Theology")

"Pigs (see Swine)," "Scriptorium," and "Incarnational
Theology" were reprinted in *The Best Spiritual Writing*
(New York: Penguin, 2010, 2012).

"Verdigris," "Kermes Red," and "Gold Leaf" appear
in *Before the Door of God: An Anthology of Devotional
Poetry* (New Haven, CT: Yale University Press, 2013).

"Crooked as a Dog's Hind Leg" and "Flat as a Flitter"
appear in *The Southern Poetry Anthology, Volume VI:
Tennessee* (Huntsville: Texas Review Press, 2013).

Melissa Range is the author of the poetry collection *Horse and Rider* (Texas Tech University Press, 2010) and the recipient of awards and fellowships from the National Endowment for the Arts, the American Antiquarian Society, the Sewanee Writers' Conference, the Fine Arts Work Center (Provincetown, MA), and the Rona Jaffe Foundation. Originally from East Tennessee, Range currently lives in Wisconsin and teaches at Lawrence University.

Tracy K. Smith is the author of three books of poetry: *The Body's Question* (2003), *Duende* (2007), and *Life on Mars* (2011), which won the 2012 Pulitzer Prize for Poetry.